Introduction

Congratulations on purchasing *Cognitive Behavioral Therapy.* Many of us are suffering with depression, anxiety, phobias, and even highly unusual forms of obsessive-compulsive disorders, not to mention several other ailments that may or may not also have something to do with the mind.

This book is meant to be a guide for using cognitive behavioral therapy to help treat the symptoms of those disorders, as well as the accompanying conditions that interfere with our daily lives. Oftentimes, we let our negative thoughts, which are more often than not irrational, intrude upon our lives and place a strain on how we live. In this book, we'll discuss the ways we can use cognitive behavioral therapy to lead a healthier, happier life.

And it isn't just you who could benefit. Children get diagnosed with anxiety and depression every day. To help our kids, we first have to understand what is going on with them. For example, children struggling with anxiety often get misdiagnosed with ADD/ADHD. The symptoms of ADD/ADHD are highly similar to symptoms of anxiety when they present in children. Anxiety and its symptoms may stem from genetics, or they may be specific situations that take place within the child's lifespan that causes its development. Oftentimes, the anxiety that a child is experiencing are due to traumatic events or irrational fears and phobias.

But it isn't always the case that there's an external reason or event that shapes the mental health of the patient. The state of one's mental health may be influenced by many different situations or by chemical imbalances within the body. Sometimes, a disorder is just a culmination of minor things or something that is inherited through the parents' genes.

Within this book, I talk about how to recognize these conditions, as well as how cognitive behavioral therapy is the best treatment for them. I give details on how to recognize and accept it when you need to seek help, along with what methods are used in addition to cognitive behavioral therapy to help treat not only mental health conditions but also negative mindsets. I also touch on strategies and techniques to help you with other goal-setting needs.

Within each chapter are several details to help you understand the conditions that are being discussed. Also included are a few statistics to help you see how rampant these conditions are in our society and what can be done to effectively treat and possibly cure them.

There are plenty of books on this subject on the market, so thanks again for choosing this one! Every effort was made to ensure it is full of as much useful information as possible. Please enjoy!

Chapter 1: What Is Cognitive Behavioral Therapy?

Cognitive Dissonance: when conflicting beliefs, behaviors, and attitudes are involved, and it produces a discomfort that leads to an altered attitude, belief system, and behaviors. This is to reduce the discomfort and try to restore balance.

Before anything else, we must first understand that all people struggle with happiness, emotional disconnect, behaviors that do not positively serve them, and negative thoughts. Cognitive behavioral therapy is a form of psychotherapy that treats these problems by finding a solution and modifying these concerns. It is not a method that involves finding the root cause and then fixing the issues; instead, cognitive behavioral therapies will focus on the solutions.

These solutions encourage and empower the patients to challenge their distorted views and thoughts and change the behaviors that lead them to self-destruction.

As with Psychiatric care you go in with a problem and the psychiatrist works on finding the root cause to that problem. They then work on developing coping mechanisms that will help you be able to cope with the trauma, or disappointments in life that you have experienced. Psychiatry is all about coping with the conditions that you have and living while maintaining the little bit of clarity that you have gained through the counseling.

 This is not always the best option for those living with mental health. Often times coping is not a great mechanism. It can often lead to alcoholism, drug use, abuse of loved ones, and sometimes suicide. Since coping is not a cure, the disorders they are trying to cope with will come back and disrupt their lives. It can cause separation between partners and even disappointment in the partner or the children that have to live with the patient.

Living with depression, anxiety, agoraphobia, OCD, anger, and many other mental health conditions have been treated with coping mechanisms for years and even though it is not the most effective tool to use, however, psychiatrist are still continuing to use it today. There has been a rise in suicides over the past thirty years and because of this there needs to be a better way to treat these disorders.

Many people suffer with trauma, depression, anxiety, anger, fear, and many other mental health conditions. With all the resources available to them you would think that help was an easy option to come by. However, it really is not easy to get help. With Cognitive Behavioral Therapy, patients are able to, not only get help that is crucial to them healing. But they also learn how to treat their conditions, not just cope with the side effects.

Treating the problem by finding valuable solutions to the symptomatic disorders is truly the best way to heal the patient. Not only do you heal the patient, but you effectively heal the family. By healing the mental health issues in one person in the family, you can begin to mend the fences that have been broken. Heal the family and start a path for the whole family to use to reach success with the symptoms and the side effects that have been caused by the years of living with a family member that is suffering.

When one person in the family suffers the rest of the family begins to suffer. Not only are they dealing with their own lives, but they are now having to live the other person's life as well, and often times picking up the slack from the family member that is struggling to cope with their disorders. Anxiety and depression can destroy the whole family. However, through Cognitive Behavioral Therapy the healing process can begin, and the family can take back their lives and begin to see a true change in the patient that has been suffering.

Cognitive Behavioral therapy can also help the whole family in group sessions that will teach each person in the family how to help the patient make better choices and live a more fulfilling life. Because of Cognitive Behavioral Therapy many people can come off of drugs, alcohol and self-loathing. They can start to make positive changes in their life which will affect their children, parents, and spouse. Treatment is out there with the proper certified Cognitive Behavioral Therapist and a proper family support system the patient can start to make positive changes that will affect their whole life.

Cognitive Behavioral Therapy: Psychotherapy that helps treat cognitive dissonance in those who suffer with finding their own solutions.

Cognitive behavioral therapy is a combination of treatments that range from psychotherapy and behavioral therapy. The psychotherapy section of cognitive behavioral therapy specifically focuses on the personal connections we feel towards events that have taken place in our childhoods. The behavioral aspect of cognitive behavioral therapy, on the other hand, specifically emphasizes the behaviors that are connected to those feelings and thoughts. That is, it focuses on the relationship that connects our problems with our thoughts and behaviors.

This type of psychotherapy is goal-oriented and hands-on, and it only takes a short time period to utilize. The goal of cognitive behavioral therapy is to alter the patterns of thinking and behaviors that are the root cause of negative behaviors, leading to changes in how the patient feels. Cognitive behavioral therapy can be used to treat many conditions in patients, including sleeping problems, anxiety, depression, drug and alcohol issues, relationship problems, and so much more.

This type of therapy works because it helps the patients change the attitudes and behaviors that have been hindering them through focusing on the thoughts behind these attitudes and behaviors. Therapists also use cognitive behavioral therapy to allow the patient to focus on the images they carry with them about their life, as well as on the beliefs and attitudes that reflect the way they deal with the emotional problems associated with the behaviors.

Most psychotherapists who use cognitive behavioral therapy are applying it in a personalized capacity for each patient. They customize the therapies used to

suit each patient's specific needs and design a
program that works best for them.

15

How long does the cognitive behavioral therapy process take?

One of the advantages of cognitive behavioral therapy is that it can take a very short span of time, within five to ten months, to produce real, lasting changes in many issues that patients have. Each session can last 50 minutes, and patients attend sessions once per week. Therapists work with the patients to build a program that can help them bring about real changes. They develop strategies and techniques that can become a set of principles they can always use to help them make changes.

How did cognitive behavioral therapy develop?

In 1960, Aaron Beck developed an understanding of how his clients were using thoughts and feelings during their therapy sessions. He experienced many sessions with clients where they have an internal dialogue that would influence their thoughts and feelings towards the situation at hand. These thoughts were not fully expressed in the sessions with his clients, and he soon realized that the thoughts the client was not expressing were the ones that were influencing their feelings. This brought about emotional changes in the clients. He coined these thoughts as automatic thoughts, which he described as emotion-filled thoughts that pop up in the mind. He also stated that people were not always fully aware of their thoughts but over time would learn to identify and then report them. Negative thoughts presented feelings of upset, and these thoughts would tend to be unrealistic and not helpful in any way. When clients were able to identify these thoughts, they make a breakthrough on how to overcome their difficulties.

Due to the importance placed on the thinking process and how the thoughts affect the patient's behavior, Beck called this process *cognitive therapy*. He then added in the "behavioral" aspect based on the behavioral techniques that are used to bring about changes not only in their behaviors but also in their cognitive thoughts. These aspects are each incorporated into the program in the specific way that is best-suited to that patient. By building a program that can be tailored to each patient, the trials that have been used for testing the validity of cognitive behavioral therapy has shown success with a wide variety of mental health problems.

Since cognitive behavioral therapy is not about the events itself but the meanings behind the events that affect us so much, negative thoughts will block us from seeing and doing things the right things, going instead with the opposite of what is true. We tend to hold on to thoughts that become a cycle of negative beliefs, and then, as humans, we fail to learn from our patterns.

Depressed individuals will think only negative thoughts, and those thoughts will manifest into actual events or situations. Oftentimes, these thoughts appeared early in the patient's childhood. They learn early on in life that to be appreciated and loved, they have to continue to do great things. It becomes a dysfunctional way of thinking, which leads them to depression, giving way to the automatic thoughts that bring about negative emotions.

When using cognitive behavioral therapy, the patients gain the ability to step outside themselves and see what is truly happening. They are able to move away from the negative thoughts and test them to verify if they are true or false. They get to see their thoughts from a different perspective, and they examine these negative thoughts from the point of view of others, seeing how other peoples' automatic thoughts have hindered or affected their lives. They are then able to take the testing even further and reveal some of their thoughts to friends and express their difficulties to them using a real-life perspective.

Although we all face negative situations or thoughts, we do not always see them as what they are— sometimes, we view them as much worse than they are.

A case study example of how cognitive behavioral therapy works

In certain situations, women find it difficult to be in social situations and as a consequence, they experience anxiety. Instead of attending social gatherings, they will isolate themselves at home. A cognitive behavioral therapist will work with the patient to educate her on what it is she is fearing and on the response that she is having. The therapist will inform her of the irrational behavior that is triggering her. The patient will learn how to shift her thoughts so that she can relax her body and utilize a plan of action that can alleviate her anxiety and calm her thoughts while engaging with others at a party. The next session, the therapist will address the steps that were used to help her with her anxiety and examine what worked, what did not offer relief, and what other methods they would like to try for this particular issue.

Cognitive behavioral therapy is used to alleviate many ailments such as anxiety, ADHD, self-esteem, depression, trauma, phobias, poor communication issues, and unrealistic expectations of your partner, but it can also be used for insomnia, anger, fear, and so many other conditions that are exacerbated by negative thoughts and behaviors. If the problems that are taking place in your life are connected to your thoughts and behaviors, then cognitive behavioral therapy is a good option to try.

Consider these questions:

- *Are you over-analyzing a past break-up?*
- *Do you spend hours online shopping even though you have no need for the particular items?*

- ***Do you constantly experience moments of negative thoughts that influence your behaviors?***

- ***Are you isolating yourself from friends and family?***

- ***Do you only feel deserving of love when you accomplish good things?***

<u>Why is cognitive behavioral therapy so popular?</u>

There have been extensive studies conducted to prove the effectiveness of cognitive behavioral therapy. Due to its direct, solution-oriented, and brief process, it has proven to make an excellent choice among those suffering from thought and behavior issues. The therapist aims to provide measurable changes in the behaviors and thoughts of the patients and produce clear results. These results can happen very quickly. Within six to ten months, you can have positive results. The patients are challenged to face what they fear and cultivate new strategies for dealing with their fears that relate to their thoughts around those fears. This empowers the patients to do something about the fears that have been limiting their ability to participate in life to the fullest. It encourages them to stop avoiding things that they find highly unpleasant.

What takes place in a cognitive behavioral therapy session?

In a cognitive behavioral therapy session, the first step is to assess the client's needs. You start out with a regular psychotherapy session where the policies of the program are discussed, along with your goals for the therapy sessions as well as the medical history of the patient. There will also be an in-depth review about the patient's concerns.

The next to be discussed are the struggles that the client is encountering and the formula that would be most effective for the response needed. Essentially, the patient will formulate a plan to overcome any situation that is preventing progress in their lives and is causing stress.

The therapist works with the patient to formulate a cognitive behavioral therapy plan that will be actionable and purposeful. The action plans they devise are to be used to identify the problems that are affecting their thoughts and behaviors. They then work on consistently making changes and develop some strategies to implement all the changes within a weeks' time. Within the action plans they design, there will also be "homework" steps to help implement those changes even outside the sessions.

<u>***What can you expect from the homework?***</u>

Because the process of cognitive behavioral therapy is meant to be quick and effective in a reduced amount of time, the goal is to provide techniques that patients can utilize throughout the entire week, whether at the therapists office or at home. These homework sessions can include:

- **Journaling**
- **Relaxation exercises**
- **Worksheets**
- **Reading**
- **Thought stopping**

Each one of these will be discussed throughout the rest of this book, and they are designed to help you transform thoughts and behaviors associated with your negative mental state.

Journaling

In the journaling process, the therapist will ask you to write about the thoughts, feelings, behaviors, and emotions that arise throughout the week. These can include those that occur during therapy sessions as well; however, you are specifically needed to journal about your feelings throughout the week as you practice your techniques outside the sessions.

Worksheets

The worksheets in the cognitive behavioral therapy homework are designed to help you target a specific area of interest. This specific homework program will help with your growth in those areas. Worksheets can be anything that the therapist designates as useful.

Reading

With the cognitive behavioral therapy homework's reading technique, you will be utilizing books that are designed to help you with your issues, and you will also be finding resources for applying a new approach to specific situations. Reading books that are geared towards self-help, cognitive behavioral therapies, and techniques to enhance your growth are all great resources that your therapist can help you find.

Relaxation exercises

Several relaxation techniques can help you with anxiety. These techniques include:

- Meditation
- Mindfulness
- Mantras

Thought stopping

With "thought stopping," your therapist will ask you to abruptly disrupt the flow of negative thoughts crowding inside your head. He or she will ask you to make a forceful statement inside your head—such as "STOP!"—which will help put a break on the thoughts and allow you to redirect the flow to more positive streams. The homework version would be to utilize this technique once every day as needed until you meet with the therapist for your next session.

How long can you expect a cognitive behavioral therapy series of sessions to last?

Due to the process of cognitive behavioral therapy and its design to be fast-acting, you can typically expect results from as short as several weeks to as long as a couple of months. Since most people are working on multiple issues in their therapy sessions, the number of issues to address and the severity of the concerns determine the actual length of time the process will take.

Brevity is also key to this approach. As one of the co-founders, Donald Meichenbaum, has suggested, with cognitive behavioral therapy, "we ask what and how questions," and they have simply found that the why question is not helpful in these types of situations.

Several techniques in the therapy sector deals with the why of your issues and concerns, instead of just simply sticking to the current thoughts and behaviors. The cognitive behavioral therapy approach is for dealing with the current thoughts and behaviors. Those wanting to know why they feel a specific way about something would need a more psychodynamic therapy approach than cognitive behavioral therapy.

Is cognitive behavioral therapy covered by most insurance plans?

While most insurance plans cover some psychotherapy or behavioral treatment programs, not all does. In the case of the ones that do, cognitive behavioral therapy should be covered. However, if you are not covered, the process could be charged anywhere from being free to $200+, based on a sliding scale and on the treatment center administering the therapy. Because of the effectiveness of the programs and techniques, the value far outweighs the cost in the long run.

What is the downside to doing cognitive behavioral therapy?

Many people find that simply exploring their experiences within a therapeutic session and generating a relationship with a therapist are not satisfying enough on their own. Since it is designed to deal directly with the symptoms and not the root cause, patients also find that the long-term relationship that can be developed with a regular therapist is not the same relationship that they would get within a cognitive behavioral therapy session. The "therapeutic" relationship that most people find with a therapist is mostly about how the latter can act as a confidant or facilitator—not as a quick, reliable problem-solver.

Since cognitive behavioral therapy is more direct and uses practicality for its techniques, it may not be helpful for those that are searching for a deep relationship with a therapist. However, since it is adjusting to the clients needs continuously, the use of modified cognitive behavioral therapies can still be beneficial within a psychotherapy framework.

Yet though the effectiveness has been found evident by test studies, some therapists who have examined this effectiveness find that it is a one-size-fits-all platform. They believe that to help the client succeed, they first need to know the root cause of the problem. They consider cognitive behavioral therapy as a short-sighted therapy program since it assumes what the client needs, and this can present a problem with those looking for other forms of treatment.

By addressing your therapist before starting, you can better assess your needs and determine if cognitive behavioral therapy is the right choice for you. With any treatment technique, feeling safe within your program is the key to success.

Most used cognitive behavioral therapy techniques

Cognitive techniques assist patients with identifying unhelpful patterns.

Cognitive techniques

These therapy techniques are designed to assist people with the ability to examine unhelpful thought patterns, as well as devise ways for them to react to problematic circumstances. The cognitive restructuring has several steps, including recording thoughts, which helps with tracking the dysfunctional automatic thoughts, allowing them to develop an adaptive response alternative. Other techniques include:

- Constructive worry
- Cognitive pie chart exercise
- Investigating thoughts
- Treating thoughts as guesses
- Acceptance exercises
- Cognitive techniques to reduce worry

- Identifying cognitive distortions like:
  - All-or-nothing thinking
  - Catastrophizing
  - Labeling
  - Fortune telling
  - Over-generalizing
  - Mind reading
  - Negative filtering

Activity scheduling

Cognitive behavioral therapy assists patients who need to engage in behaviors they would not normally engage in. This technique entails identifying the lower frequency behaviors, then allotting time throughout the week to schedule those behaviors and increase their frequency. Examples include:

- Identifying behavioral causes of depression
- Behavioral activation

Graded exposure

This cognitive behavioral therapy is structured to reduce the anxiety and fear or phobias that the patient has. This can be achieved through exposing patients to their fear or phobia.

This has been considered one of the most useful and effective cognitive behavioral therapy techniques. The theory behind this technique is that the avoidance of things patients most fear only serves to increase the fear and anxiety. With this therapy, the goal is to systematically approach the things feared the most in a calculated manner and thus, significantly reduce the level of fear.

Successive approximation

This therapy will help those who suffer with overwhelming goals in tackling them and succeeding. The key is to break the large tasks systematically into smaller, more digestible tasks. They can also group together similar tasks, which may or may not be related, to complete them in one go and reduce the difficulty. This allows them to gain a mastery of the skills that will be needed to achieve the larger, more complicated goals.

Mindfulness meditation

This cognitive behavioral therapy helps patients disengage from the harmful thoughts they are ruminating or obsessing over. Using this technique, they learn to connect with the present time period as well as practice forms of meditation. This method is the subject of a significant quantity of recent research whose results show how effective it is with psychological problems. Variants of this method include:

- Mindfulness "what" skills
- Mindfulness "how" skills
- Finding wise mind
- Mindfulness exercises for stress reduction
- Mindfulness half-smile exercise
- Mindfulness exercises for chronic pain

Skills training assists with remedies for skill deficits.

Skills training

This cognitive behavioral therapy is designed to help remedy skill deficits, which allows the patient to work through the directions, the modeling, and the role-playing. The most targeted during skills training are communication training, assertiveness training, and social skills training. Another example is called "validating difficult people."

Problem-solving assists in finding a solution to problems.

Problem-solving

This exercise helps the patients in their quest for finding a solution. This can work well with chronic mood issues and repeated disappointments, allowing the patients to take a passive role when the difficult circumstances arise. By teaching problem-solving strategies, the patients are able to regain control of their issues and maintain their situation.

Relaxation breathing training assists in reducing the physiological symptoms of anxiety.

Relaxation breathing training

This form of cognitive behavioral therapy can best be described as a technique that reduces the physiological symptoms that are associated with anxiety. These can be shortness of breath, dizziness, rapid heartbeat, and many more. With the reduction in anxiousness, the patients are able to think more clearly, allowing them to increase their comfort levels and actively lower their anxiety levels further.

Chapter 2: Relieving Anxiety with Cognitive Behavioral Therapy

What exactly is anxiety?

Anxiety affects more than 40 million adults in the USA alone. The average age of people with anxiety is 31 years old, but some are even younger. Anxiety has been found in kids as young as 10, with the age group of 13-18 making up a large portion of the sufferers.

Anxiety: panic attacks, incapacitating phobias, obsessive thoughts, and unrelenting worries.

If you experience panic attacks, unrelenting worries, incapacitating phobias, and obsessive thoughts, then you may be suffering from an anxiety disorder. Several subtypes make up the umbrella of Anxiety Disorders, such as:

- Generalized anxiety disorder
- Panic disorder

- Social anxiety
- Post-traumatic stress disorder
- Agoraphobia, or other specific phobias
- Obsessive-compulsive disorder

Anxiety can affect not only the mental well-being of a patient but also their physical well-being. The physical symptoms include:

- Panic attacks
- Shortness of breath
- Shaking
- Nausea
- Headache
- Rapid heartbeat
- Dizzy spells

Due to the prevalence of anxiety in children and young adults, it has become the most common form of disability in the USA. Approximately 10% of those under the age of 20 and 40% of adults over the age of 21 suffer from anxiety. Although there are many treatment options within the mental health community, two-thirds of suffers never seek treatment. Teens are the least-treated subgroup, with only 1 in 5 teens who are suffering receiving intervention. Due in part to chemical imbalances in the human body, more and more people suffering from anxiety each day. However, the leading cause of anxiety is not yet known.

One other fact about anxiety sufferers is that men are less likely to be diagnosed than women. Similarly, we also see war veterans who suffer from PTSD—which includes flashbacks from their deployments—go without treatment. Another very common group of anxiety sufferers include those who are victims of domestic violence, accidents, natural disasters, sexual abuse, and child abuse.

Although anxiety has several forms, there are many that people do not recognize as such, including phobias and panic attacks, which can leave the sufferer debilitated and experiencing intense pain, causing them to avoid the fear or phobia completely. This can lead to staying in a tightly controlled space or never leaving their house.

A condition closely connected to anxiety is OCD. This is a mania or compulsion which may take specific forms like trichotillomania, pyromania, and germaphobia, among others. These are characterized by continuous, uncontrollable urges that incite the patient to start fires, pull their hair out, obsessively clean their homes, or wash their hands excessively for fear of germs.

A standard person suffering with anxiety will also present with symptoms of depression and other conditions. Anxiety is usually developed by those who experience a traumatic event or environmental stresses. However, many people who have not experienced any of these can also be afflicted with this mental illness.

How does anxiety affect children?

Children who suffer from anxiety can exhibit symptoms of OCD. They usually do not have the capacity yet to realize that the obsessive and compulsive behaviors that arise due to their anxieties can be controlled or treated. They experience intrusive thoughts that will invade their minds and demand that they complete ritualistic tasks or complete a routine to ease their anxiety.

It is often found that children between the ages of 8 and 12 suffer with OCD-related anxieties, which can also increase as they move into their teen years and early adult years. It is often a problem that goes misdiagnosed among kids or else goes undiagnosed altogether. There is an estimate that 1 in 200 children and 1 in 20 teens suffer from anxiety-related OCD. Most teens with OCD are often misunderstood. Their academics can become affected, and they may end up living a lifestyle full of torment. They can appear to be distracted, distanced, daydreaming, lazy, or disinterested completely. They may also seem to be completely unfocused or have difficulty with their concentration levels. Oftentimes, this is because they have nagging urges that are distracting them from being able to focus. They are confused by the urges, and it creates a stressful environment for them. This can sometimes be very terrifying for the students, especially those who have horrific OCD thoughts or images running through their heads. The distraction could be due to them trying to focus on the rituals they need to complete, and they either covertly or overtly need to relieve the distress.

This can be frustrating to the students as well as the administrators of their school, and it can create difficulties even in their home environment. These anxiety disorders can sometimes be misdiagnosed due to the similarities they have to other mental health disorders. Since a ritual that only happens in the mind and doesn't have physical manifestations cannot be observed, the children that are suffering can wax and wane over time and sometimes even exhibit no symptoms, making them even more difficult to track.

By introducing cognitive behavioral therapy early in life, there may be a better chance of treating those suffering with OCD-related anxiety by rewiring the brain.

How cognitive behavioral therapy can help those who suffer with anxiety

With cognitive behavioral therapy, the patient is able to make sense of all the challenging situations that will arise and control his or her problematic reactions to them. This therapy can emphasize three components:

- Thoughts
- Behaviors

- Emotions

The patient and therapist would start by breaking down the difficult feelings within these parts, and as they proceed, they should have a clearer idea on where and how they should intervene.

They will re-examine a negative thought that is causing a chain reaction of negative emotions, as well as behaviors. If they find that there is a behavioral problem causing the reaction, then they will find a new behavioral answer for the current situation. The therapy exercises are designed to intertwine with the three components and create a solution.

For instance, if you are experiencing uncontrollable worry, then cognitive behavioral therapy exercises should help you identify the thoughts and become grounded. In time, you will reduce the emotion of anxiety, and it will ultimately make engagement in the behavior easier, as it addresses the problematic circumstances and starts the chain reaction.

Techniques to exercise cognitive behavior therapy treatments

Cognitive therapy

Looks at the negative thought patterns and examines how they contribute to the patient's anxiety.

Behavioral therapy

Looks at the way a patient behaves or reacts to a situation that triggers their anxiety.

Anxiety is triggered by our thoughts, not by external situations or events. The perception of each situation will determine how the patient feels, and it can, in fact, increase the anxiety. For instance, let's say you are invited to a party. In each scenario, you will experience different emotions.

Scenario 1: The party sounds fun, and you would love to go and meet new people.
Emotions are *happy* and *excited*.

Scenario 2: **Parties are not something you like to do. You would rather stay home and watch a movie. Emotions are neutral.**

Scenario 3: **You never fit in at parties. You do not have anything to talk about. You will make a fool of yourself. You're not going.**
Emotions are *anxious* **and** *sad.*

Each scenario is dealing with the same premise; however, in the last scenario, you are experiencing anxiety from a simple invite to a party. This is how anxiety can affect your whole life. Although you might really want to go to the party, the anxiety and thoughts that you have tell you that you are not good at parties and you would rather be at home.

Cognitive behavioral therapy steps

Identifying the negative thought patterns

Anxiety disorder can cause the sufferer to perceive a situation as more dangerous than most other people would perceive it. For instance, a person who has germaphobia will perceive shaking someone's hand as life-threatening. These are irrational fears, and being able to identify them is the first step. Start by asking yourself what other thoughts you were having when this thought came up. Your therapist will walk you through several steps to help you with this.

Challenging thoughts that are negative

Next, your therapist will help you by teaching you how to evaluate the thoughts that are anxiety-provoking. In this stage, you will question your frightening thoughts with evidence and analyze the beliefs that are unhelpful while testing them in a real-life situation with a predictable negative thought pattern.

You will conclude experiments, determine the chances of the anxiety being realistic, and weight the differences between the worrying and the avoiding with pros and cons. Then you will examine what would happen if the anxiety was not there.

Replace your unrealistic negative thoughts with realistic positive thoughts

After working to identify the unrealistic, irrational predictions and distortions of negative, anxious thoughts, you will then be taught how to replace them with new thoughts that are more accurate. These thoughts will have a positive pattern. Your therapist can also assist you with calming statements that are realistic in nature. These statements will be something that you can say to yourself when you have to face a situation that would normally incite anxiety.

Examples for replacing negative thought with a more realistic thought pattern:

What if I pass out while riding in on a bus? → Assuming the worst-case version of the situation would occur.

Realistically, the patient has never passed out while riding the bus, so this situation is unlikely to happen. *If I do pass out, it will be horrible for me.* → Making things seem bigger than they actually are.

Realistically, if the patient faints, they will likely be revived in a few minutes, and it will not be that horrible.

People will think I am a druggy or a crazy person. → Making assumptions of what other people think of you.

Realistically, people will more than likely be more concerned about your health than what kind of person you are; they may not even think too deeply about it.

Some more steps that can be taken with cognitive behavioral therapy include:

- Recognizing the signs that trigger anxiety or that the symptoms are about to surface.

- Being able to apply coping skills in times of crisis.

- Facing the fears so that you are more familiar with how different from your imaginings things would actually play out in reality.

Chapter 3: Relieving Depression with Cognitive Behavioral Therapy

Depression: Long-lasting sadness that is overwhelming; energy levels that do not permit you to participate in activities; appetite reduction that becomes detrimental to your health; and your interest levels in things that used to be your favorite activities decreases to the point of non-existence.

Depression is one of the most diagnosed condition in America today. The leading type of depression among people between the ages of 15 and 44 is called major depressive disorder. A recent estimate, it affects 16.1 million American adults.

This means that 6.7% of US citizens aged 18 and up are diagnosed with depression. Although this disorder can develop at any age, the average person is diagnosed around age 32, and these numbers are mostly found in women.

Another form of depression is called persistent depressive disorder, also known as PPD. This type of depression, which used to be called dysthymia, can persist for a minimum of two years. It has been approximated that it affects 1.5% of US citizens age 18 and above. That equates to 3.3 million people In America alone. They have also found that the average age of diagnoses is 31.

With depression being the leading cause of disability among children and adults worldwide, it is no wonder we are studying new services and treatments that can alleviate or cure the illnesses. The persisting problem is that about 75% of the diagnosed cases are not receiving any treatment, especially in developing countries. This results in an average of 1 million people who take their lives each year.

What is depression and how can we recognize it?

Depression can be identified by a number of its resulting symptoms. Most of us have experienced grief; however, it should not last more than a few days, except grief from the loss of a loved one. A major depressive disorder is more than just a mild case of grief. It is classified as a mood disorder that lasts longer than a few days or even weeks.

These symptoms are long-lasting and can be recognized by sadness that is overwhelming, energy levels that do not permit you to participate in any form of life's activities, appetite reduction that becomes detrimental to your health, and your interest levels in things that used to be your favorite activities decreases to the point of non-existence.

There is said to be an estimated 16.2 million American adults, or roughly 6.7% of the population, who have been diagnosed with at least one episode of major depressive disorder within one year's time. Depression can lead to many other health-related conditions, and it can place a person's life at risk.

Types of depressive disorders

Persistent depressive disorder

This can mean a single episode of depression as well as recurring episodes. Also known as dysthymia, persistent depressive disorder is a chronic depressive condition that is low-level. The severity of the depression is lower than major depressive disorder, which can last two or more years. It can be characterized by ongoing symptoms of hopelessness, or sadness, along with other conditions such as energy reduction and indecisiveness. This happens to 1.5 million Americans every year. Women are more likely to be diagnosed when it comes to this sort of depression, and many cases are considered serious.

Bipolar disorder

This form of depressive disorder was once called manic-depressive disorder. It has been reported to affect 2.8% of American citizens every year. The balance is equal between men and women on who it affects, and 83% of the cases diagnosed each year are rated as severe. How can you recognize bipolar disorder? The patients will often present with manic mood episodes, which are energized states of excitement and over-activity that are then preceded by episodes of extreme low mood, or depression. If the patient is experiencing these fluctuating moods, then this would be the diagnosis they would receive.

Seasonal depressive disorder

If you are experiencing moods that are affected by the seasons changing, then you will probably be diagnosed with seasonal affective disorder. This condition is roughly said to affect 5% of the American population each year. This is usually brought on by an autumn or winter seasonal change and is very rarely seen in summer and spring seasonal changes. Your geographical location, as well as the location's distance from the equator, can play a significant part in your condition. More women than men are diagnosed with this type of depressive disorder, usually 4 out of 5.

Post-partum depressive disorder

Also known as the baby blues, post-partum depressive disorder's symptoms will present as mood swings, lack of sleep, and sadness. These symptoms should pass within 2 weeks; if they do not, seek medical help. Post-partum depressive disorder can be a hormonal imbalance associated with childbirth. The lack of sleep that new mothers receive is another likely reason. The new stresses of a baby in the home and responsibilities of another person can cause post-partum to develop.

If you experience the symptoms longer than a few weeks or if you see that the symptoms are getting worse, it could be major depressive disorder with a peripartum onset, which is also considered to be post-partum depression. There are several other symptoms that you can look for such as withdrawal, appetite reduction, and thoughts that are negative and evasive. Roughly 10 to 15% of all American new mothers experience some form of this depression within 3 months of delivery. Of new fathers, 10% will also experience these symptoms. This is considered a family disease, and when left without treatment, it can affect the children as well.

Psychotic depressive disorder

This form of major depressive disorder is accompanied by delusions, paranoia, and hallucinations. This would be classified as major depressive disorder with psychotic features. This type of depressive disorder can affect on average 25% of the patients that are seen by hospitals and 1 in 13 people in the world will experience the psychotic episodes before 75.

What can be done to help?

Cognitive behavioral therapy is making great strides in treating most depressive disorders. With depression comes negative thinking, and cognitive behavioral therapy can help with adjusting those negative thoughts. Several techniques are used to reframe these thoughts. There are also several forms of negative thoughts. Below is a list of the most prevalent negative thought patterns that are present in those undergoing cognitive behavioral therapy.

- Thinking that is all-or-nothing

- Focusing on only the negative

- Self-labeling negatively

- Catastrophizing everything

- Needing approval excessively

- "Should" statements

- Pessimism

- Worrying too much about the past

- Forgetting to be in the present for fear of not getting things done

- Making assumptions about other people's opinions of yourself

Cognitive behavioral therapy can help will all of these troublesome thought processes. It is a technique that helps you talk about what you think of other people, what you think they think of you, and how you view the world. This technique helps you examine how the things you do will affect how you feel and think in the long run.

It assists you in changing the way you think, which is the cognitive aspect, and then alter the way you act, which is the behavioral aspect. With these changes, you will be able to feel more happiness in life and notice changes in your mental health. Cognitive behavioral therapy focuses only on the present: the here and now. It focuses on the problems that you are faced with today and the difficulties you are experiencing in the moment. The techniques used will help with an improved state of mind for the present, not the past.

How does it work?

Cognitive behavioral therapy is designed to help you make more sense of the overwhelming problems that are persistent in your life. The techniques break down all the steps into small parts, making it easier for the patient to see how things are connected and how those actions and thoughts affect you.

For instance:

- A situation—events, problems, or difficult situations that take place in your life.

Then the techniques help you assess how they can affect your:

- Emotions
- Thoughts
- Physical feelings
- Actions

That is, the way you feel about specific problems, and the thoughts that surround those problems will affect the physical and emotional feelings towards those problems. This will, in turn, alter what you do and how you do it. You can react in a positive way that is helpful or a negative way that is harmful. It all depends on the thoughts that present in your mind about the situation.

Since the effects of negative thinking can affect your recovery from depression, it is obviously very important to get the negative thinking under control. Negative thoughts will keep you in a depressed state of mind. Current research has found that although depression is a negative, sad state of mind, the patients who are depressed are not lacking a positive mindset, they simply block themselves from feeling the positive feelings. They self-sabotage themselves to stay depressed longer. They dampen their senses by making blanket statements such as, "I don't deserve to be this happy." For instance, a post-partum mother who tells herself that she doesn't deserve to get better since she is a bad mother for having post-partum. It becomes an endless cycle that keeps them in the depressed state. By utilizing cognitive behavioral therapy, they can begin to regain some control over their thoughts and start to heal.

How does it help those that are depressed?
By working with a certified therapist trained in the application of cognitive behavioral therapy, the patient can work to change patterns of behavior that needs to be changed. The main goal is to use these steps to recalibrate the brain so that the patient can then retain happy thoughts without any negative thoughts blocking them.

The patient and the therapist will work together to put into perspective any reactions that cause the dampening of the thoughts into negative thoughts. There will be regular work done within the therapeutic sessions and outside the sessions for a reinforced pattern change. Patients have found that recognizing their negative thought patterns is quite liberating.

The following are five techniques to counteract the negative thoughts in those who are depressed through the use of cognitive behavioral therapy.

1. Finding the problem and then brainstorming with a therapist for a solution.

2. Counteracting the negative thoughts with self-statements. It's a rewriting of the negative thoughts into positive ones.

3. Using every new opportunity to use a positive thought.

4. At the end of the day, using visualization to see the day as its best parts. Write those things that you are most thankful for that day and show gratitude for the blessings you have.

5. Letting disappointment become a normal part of life instead of a depressing state of being. Accepting disappointment is empowering.

Chapter 4: Reframing Your Mindset and Phobias with Cognitive Behavioral Therapy

Phobias are classified as extreme fear that is connected to a specific situation or tangible object that can result in highly avoidable behaviors. These behaviors are displayed with a severe sign of distress when confronted with specific objects that have been feared, as well as situations that can disrupt the day to day living of the person.

Phobias: fears that are irrational and prevent you from participating in life activities.

If the phobia is preventing you from working or fulfilling other life responsibilities, as well as from performing tasks necessary for a balanced lifestyle or health, then it should be addressed immediately. This can affect the interpersonal relationships that this person has. Many people will simply avoid the triggers to their phobias. However, this can limit their ability to live a full life. If the phobia you are dealing with is not a detriment to your health, then you could simply choose to forego the cost of cognitive behavioral therapy and avoid the phobias instead.

Many of these types of anxiety disorders are in fact curable, but this does not mean that any one treatment plan can work for all phobias. Each person is unique and different in the way they handle their conditions and treatment plans. Each time someone goes in for treatment, the method can be completely different from each other. The therapist will devise a program that works best for you.

When using cognitive behavioral therapy for the treatment of phobias, you are able to manage the fears and gradually modify the way you process those thoughts. This is completely designed for interconnectedness of beliefs with thoughts, feelings, and behaviors.

How does a phobia work inside the mind?

Someone suffering with phobias will find a situation fearful as if it is inherently dangerous, even if the fear is unfounded. This belief will lead the patient to have negative automatic thought processes. These can occur in many fearful situations that are encountered on a daily basis: the cognitive thoughts will react with a phobic instead of an appropriate response. These are called phobic behavioral reactions.

How does the therapist facilitate the healing process?

With several sessions, the therapist will help you overcome these fears using steps that are incremental. A good example of how the therapist will work with cognitive behavioral therapy to treat dogs fear to start with some reading material about dogs and interactions with dogs. Then they will move on to watching movies with dogs, and lastly, they will bring you in front of a puppy for harmless dog interactions.

The techniques that are involved in cognitive behavioral therapy can be drawn from therapeutic treatments such as the school of behaviorism as well as learning theory. They will also draw techniques from the school of cognitive theory. Each one provides steps that will help move the patient forward and away from their irrational fears and phobias.

Another method used within the cognitive behavioral therapy model is the process of group therapy. This involves multiple people with the same or similar phobias coming together to talk about their fears, their progress, and what is working and what isn't working in their treatment. These people will assemble for what is typically called a conference, where they will learn to face their fears head-on and where they will engage in psychoeducational classes that will expose the group to the exact fear or phobia.

If group therapies are not an option, they can also use individual therapy as a method for helping the patients reach a comfortable level with their fears or phobias. This allows individual focus on the patient form the therapists. They will build some rapport towards each other, and this will put the patient at ease so that they can work in a safe, friendly environment for the patient's best interest. Even though this is a good process for some, others might not benefit from this method. With cognitive behavioral therapies, the patient can quickly produce results.

Family therapy is another treatment plan that can be included in the cognitive behavioral therapy treatment plan. If the therapist feels like the family dynamic is a contributing factor to the phobia or that they can be a benefit to the progress, he or she may include family therapies into the treatment plan. The therapist will facilitate one of the communication sessions with the family members and the patient, allowing the family and patient to address the fear as best as they can. This works really well with children who are experiencing phobias.

There are also medication programs that can be incorporated into the cognitive behavioral therapy treatment plan. These can include medications such as:

- Beta-blockers

- Antidepressants

- SSRIs

- Sedatives

SSRIs and antidepressants are medicines that will act on the serotonin levels present in your brain. Serotonin is the chemical in place when you experience happiness.

Types of phobias associated with the use of cognitive behavioral therapy

There are several forms of phobias which can be treated by cognitive behavioral therapy. Each one has a unique fingerprint on how it responds and what symptoms that they bring out in the patient. Below is a list of those phobias and some information to help you understand what they are.

Simple phobias

This particular phobia classification can be associated with the fear of specific objects and situations. These can include but are not limited to, heights, dark, small objects, moths, ice cream, balloons, bridges, and so on. This is considered the least restrictive phobia.

Agoraphobia

This fear is most closely associated with the need to be able to escape any area quickly, as well as the ability to find help if something goes wrong. This can include panic disorders. With agoraphobia, you can be fearful of a large variety of things. These are situations or things that the patient believes will incapacitate or reduce their ability to reach help if they need to. This can include shopping at the mall, being alone in general, or even using a public transportation system. This is considered the most crippling phobia.

Social phobia

This particular phobia can be associated best with the fear of others watching you or evaluating what you are doing. It is also associated with the belief that others will indeed think that the sufferer is being foolish and acting strange, when in fact they are not. This will bring about avoidance of others in situations where others will be involved, such as eating, dancing, parties, meetings, and any other social interaction.

Those who suffer with a phobia will most likely present them in childhood and will suffer with chronic issues of anxiety and depression. It is said that simple phobias can develop in childhood, while social phobia and agoraphobia can develop in the late teens to mid-20's, depending on the patient's mental health. Females, rather than males, will be more prone to phobias, except in the case of social phobias where both sexes suffer about equally.

What can cause phobias?

Many therapists believe that phobias are a simple

conditioning from an experience that was traumatic,

within a specific time, situation, or around a specific

object. This can be something as serious as a

traumatic injury from being bitten by a dog, or a

traumatic event that took place in a car. But although

this is thought to be the root cause, this is not always

the case. Simple phobias and social phobias often take

place due to social situations, or they occur internally.

This can be attributed to the passing of false or

exaggerated information within families and friends,

as well as with watching someone else be injured in a

similar manner to what you believe to be fearful or dangerous.

How does Cognitive behavioral therapy help with the treatment of phobias?

By helping the patients understand the fears and how they connect to their life, they are able to learn how to overcome them as well as how to handle them when they arise. This helps them to no longer be limited by their fears and phobias.

Conditioning

Many phobias can be considered the result of conditioning, such as how Pavlov conditioned his dog to salivate when a bell was rung. This means that over time, the patient has experienced the actions that created the phobia over and over again until it became almost a fixture.

Inheriting

Many of our fears can be inherited in our DNA from our parents. They will instill fears into us by creating the phobias. Mothers who are overly fearful during the gestation period will pass on the high fear level into their children. This has been proven in several studies. Oftentimes as a parent, we can recognize signs in our children that remind us of ourselves or of our emotions while carrying that child. For instance, if you are very angry during your pregnancy, you will find that your child is very angry. If you eat lots of cheeseburgers during pregnancy, your child is most likely going to love cheeseburgers.

Treatments for phobias using cognitive behavioral therapy

Treatments for phobias can vary. However, when cognitive behavioral therapy is involved, you will first identify the fear and then tailor the treatment that is necessary to enable the change that you are wishing to make. They can then alter, reduce, or modify the behaviors or symptoms that come from the fear.

The treatment can be utilized by learning the nature of the fear. Then they will work towards the cognitive phase that will introduce different thoughts along with an altered perception of the object or situation that is most feared. The next step would be to allow a systematic exposure to the object or situation that is feared the most.

The end result leads the patient to associate the previously viewed negative fear towards an object or situation into a positive perception. Oftentimes, the use of cognitive behavioral therapy will lead the patient to a significant reduction in symptoms in 10-20 sessions.

Chapter 5: Living a Happy Life by Utilizing Cognitive Behavioral Therapy

Now that we have discussed cognitive behavioral therapy and all the steps that patients and therapists can take to alleviate symptomatic depression, anxiety, negative mindset, and phobias, we can talk about living a happy life through the use of cognitive behavioral therapy.

To live a happy, fulfilling life, you will need to change your negative, unrealistic, irrational thoughts into a positive, more realistic, rational thought pattern. To start with, you need to admit and recognize that you have irrational-negative thoughts and rational-positive thoughts. Each one is formed a bit differently, and examples include:

- Irrational-negative thoughts

- o *I'm definitely going to have a bad day since it is raining outside.*
  - o *I should have never been born, then my parents would not argue and be on the verge of divorce.*
  - o *I am going to be late for work and get fired because this guy just hit my bumper. I'm not going to be able to pay for a new one. I'm such a screw-up, and nothing ever goes right for me.*
- Rational-positive thoughts
  - o *The flowers are going to be blooming now that it is raining. They really needed the water.*
  - o *Although my parents are arguing a lot, their arguments are not because of me. I will show them love and support and help them resolve their differences without guilt.*
  - o *I am so grateful that no one is hurt in this accident. Although my bumper is damaged, it could have been worse.*

Although therapy is part of the cognitive behavioral therapy process, we must remember that "therapy" here is not about the therapist doing the work for you. It involves asking lots of questions. You must get comfortable with asking questions and then looking for the answers from within, Some of these questions can include:

- What are the reasons behind your thought that you will never be happy?
- What evidence do you have that supports this thought?
- Have you ever asked an individual you liked on a date?
- How often are you rejected when you put yourself out there?
- How often are you *not* rejected?

There are three types of problems that we face every day.

There is the practical: This is the situation which presents itself when you are trying to accomplish a goal, but there is an obstacle.

There is the emotional: This is the reaction to the situation.

There is the imagined: This is the situation that you invented in your mind.

For example:

The practical problem would be your car breaking down.
The emotional reaction would be that you get upset.

Although most people's reaction to their car breaking down would be getting upset, the actual car breaking down is not the cause of you being upset. Instead, you are upset due to your reaction to the situation.

In situations where you are experiencing emotional upsets, ask yourself, is the problem a matter of "want" or "need"?

Want is something you desire. Need is something that connects to basic survival. This includes air, food, water, or medication.

Do you *need* the car to not break down? Does it threaten your basic survival? No, probably not. However, you want it to not break down because it makes your life easier and it's less expensive this way. Reacting with a gut reaction is not going to help the situation, and it doesn't change the problem. It simply feeds into the negative thoughts that come up. It is an irrational reaction to a rational situation. So, by changing your thinking processes, you are able to live a happier life.

When people suffer with irrational-negative thoughts, they spend the majority of their lives in an unconscious state of being. They do not realize these things are irrational and negative because they do not know anything else. They think that what they feel and think are just normal processes that everyone else also goes through. However, their thoughts and their mind are slowly killing them.

After they recognize that they are having these irrational-negative thoughts, they then have to admit to themselves exactly to what degree they are experiencing them. They also need to admit to themselves that their thoughts are irrational-negative thoughts, and think about how often they occur. Are these happening once or twice a day or more often than not? Admitting the truth to yourself is the most important step to being able to change them and deal with the thoughts.

With a bit of help from your therapist and by doing homework like the ones I will list below, you can help change your thoughts. These actions will change your life for the better, so following them is key to making changes.

First, each time you start feeling depressed or anxious, take out your journal and write down the thoughts that pass through your mind.

Later, you will need to analyze all of these thoughts. Which ones are irrational-negative thoughts? How many of them are irrational-negative thoughts? Change these thoughts into rational-positive thoughts. Write down your rational-positive thoughts.

To make these changes, you will need to write them down every single day. This will help you eliminate those debilitating thoughts and change your irrational-negative thoughts to rational-positive thoughts automatically.

For a while, you will simply write those thoughts down on paper and change them into rational-positive thoughts. Eventually, over time, your ability to change them will become automatic, and this will be a shock when you do it the first time. That day that you stop yourself and automatically change the pattern of thoughts will be the one where you begin to change your life. Each time you do it, you will find that it gets easier and easier. Over time, it becomes second nature to you. At this point, you will have taken back the control of your life and mind. This will be an impactful moment in your life.

A few more advantages that come with the use of cognitive behavioral therapy when improving your life and living happier are listed below.

Greater presence: Cognitive behavioral therapy based on mindfulness can help you be more present for your friends and family. Mindfulness training has been known to increase the practitioner's ability to be more attentive to those that we care about. By using cognitive behavioral therapy, the patient is able to translate the need to be present into an action plan that will make it happen. For instance, the next time you are discussing something with your partner, consider bringing your undivided full attention to the conversation. Listen intently to everything they are saying. Practice listening as if this is the first time you have ever seen this person. Focus deeply on what they are saying.

Less anxiety: Living with anxiety can also take a toll on your partner due to the constant need for a support system they can provide. Oftentimes, those suffering with anxiety need a "safety companion," or someone that can help in times of panic disorder or agoraphobic episodes. For instance, when you have panic attacks, the other person has to rearrange their schedules to accommodate your needs. This can place undue strain on the relationship. It can lead to resentment and irritability. With cognitive behavioral therapy, the relief of the anxiety will help the relationship improve since the anxiety is no longer controlling the schedule and damaging the relationship. Next time you are having uncontrollable anxiety, consider finding a therapist that is certified in cognitive behavioral therapy.

Improved mood: Depression can weigh on the family of the person who suffers it. It is hard for the one suffering to be enthusiastic about life or activities, they have low or no energy, and the sex drive, among other things, decreases drastically. With cognitive behavioral therapy over a 12- to 16-week time period, patients can start to feel better. They will gain their ability to function without the decreased energy, their sex drive will improve, their enthusiasm for life will increase, and they will find more excitement in their activities. When the individual is suffering, the whole family suffers; when they are happy, the whole family is happy. So consider using cognitive behavioral therapy either on your own or with a trained therapist and see how well it can improve your life.

Better sleep: Twenty-three percent of adults in America suffer with bad sleep habits. When you do not get enough time to sleep, you will display irritability, impatience, and crankiness, and your personal interactions with family and friends can become shaky. Insomnia has been known to turn your bedtime into stress time. This blocks the coziness of your bed and places you in an uncomfortable state for the whole night. It can even interfere with your partner's sleep patterns. Cognitive behavioral therapy can help with insomnia in 4 to 6 sessions. It can help a person regain the ability to fall asleep as well as sleep more soundly. It also helps restore the connection between their bed and rest and relaxation instead of stress. Consider cognitive behavioral therapy for your sleep-improvement needs.

Healthier relationship with alcohol: Drinking too much can be unhealthy for your health and your relationships. There is a higher divorce rate among those that over-use alcohol than any other concern. It is also tied to the violence of partners and dissatisfaction among those in a relationship with an alcohol abuser. Cognitive behavioral therapy is a great way to target those thoughts and behaviors that fuels the alcohol problem, and it helps the sufferer find a better way of coping with their alcohol use. Oftentimes, couples behavioral therapy is the most effective treatment. This is where both partners participate with the treatment plan. Since alcohol abuse is so severe, a life-long abstinence is necessary for continued success. There are treatment programs that will work towards a modest alcohol consumption, but in general, abstinence is best.

Happier kids: When children are suffering with phobias or anxiety, it can affect the whole family. Parents will suffer along with the child because they feel the strain from the child's refusal to participate in the activity they fear. There is a saying that rings true in this case, "You are only as happy... as your least happy child." With each set of parents, there is a vast difference in parenting styles. One can be lenient, and one can be strict. Since the child is causing undue stress, the symptoms can amplify the parenting styles. This leads to conflict within the home wherein parents bicker back and forth about the proper way to care for that child, leading to resentment and anger between the two parents. Cognitive behavioral therapy, along with behavioral treatments, has been found to be quite useful in these childhood disorders. They can help all parties involved, not just the child. Consider trying cognitive behavioral therapy with your child, both in your own home and in a therapist's office.

Healthier patterns of thought: Cognitive behavioral therapy is not only used for mental health but for relationships and for communication as well. Since it is based on the connection between behaviors, thoughts, and feelings, to have reality-aligned thoughts means we will have a more positive behaviors and feelings. The negative-irrational thoughts that enter our minds can be detrimental to our relationships. An example could be how your spouse continues to leave their clothes in the middle of the floor when they take them off. You, in turn, think, "he must think I'm his maid since he just throws his clothes in the floor. He doesn't care about me and all the things I have to do throughout the day. He must think he works harder and doesn't have to clean up after himself. He doesn't value my work or my help in the home." These are all irrational-negative thoughts; there's no proof that they are valid. These types of thoughts interfere with the relationship and can end up driving a wedge between the two partners.

In cognitive behavioral therapy, the patient is supposed to notice the thoughts that we are continuously telling ourselves. They often happen so quickly and automatic that we do not even have time to connect the story in our mind to a real situation that took place. Once you are able to identify those thoughts, you can begin to change them into rational-positive thoughts. Maybe your partner throwing his clothes to the floor has no bearing on how he thinks of your services—maybe he simply is too tired and complacent to pick them up. His preoccupation could have nothing to do with your relationship status at all. Maybe your worries are more specific to a concern you are having from some other situation, and in that situation, it is a warranted feeling.

Cognitive behavioral therapy is not a treatment plan that advocates lying to the psyche. However, it is a treatment plan that helps us edit those negative thoughts into a more accurate positive thought.

Ask yourself these questions when you get upset with your spouse, friends, or family:

- What is the proof for the thought that I had?
- Is the proof contrary to my thoughts?
- Based on this proof, how accurate are my thoughts?
- How will I modify this thought to reflect a more realistic thought about the situation?

Intentions are enacted greater: We all want to be attentive to our partners. We want to be supportive, patient, and generous. As with any relationship, we have paved it with the best of intentions. However, if we are not deliberate with our values, then we risk leaving our intentions as mere platitudes that are vague and without any substance. For instance, telling ourselves that family is the most important, then living completely opposite of that and placing them last. Cognitive behavioral therapy can be used even though you do not have a disorder to address. It is a great tool to use for sustaining action that is supported by our values.

By taking inventory of your relationships and setting a clearly defined goal about them, you can begin to fix those relationships. For example, planning to turn your phone off during meal time and communicating with your family instead. Collaborating with your family to help make this change is a great way to get everyone on board. A cognitive behavioral therapy program would include activities that are planned so that you stay on a specific path, such as placing action steps into a calendar. For instance, you can place "spend time with the kids doing something they love to do" into a calendar. The next step would be to protect that time slot from any other distractions.

Consider having a conversation with your partner and seeing who they need you to be for the relationship to work. Then plan to move towards the goals set. Take note of any effects that happen within the relationship.

The positive message about cognitive behavioral therapy: The most important message that you can take away from this book is that although many people will say that you cannot control your thoughts and actions, this is absolutely not true. You have complete control over your thoughts and actions. You were the one that created the thoughts, and that means you can change them.

The basic understanding of cognitive behavioral therapy is that you have all the control in how you think and behave. When you are faced with situations that present negative thoughts, remember that you are the one placing those thoughts into your head. So simply tell yourself, "STOP!" and rewrite your thoughts to be more positive instead of negative.

It can be quite hard to edit your thinking patterns. This is because you have conditioned yourself to believe these thoughts. So by being patient and by practicing the homework assigned by your therapist, you can begin to make true changes in your life and thought processes. It may be uncomfortable at first, but it will get easier and easier. All it needs is practice. Imagine using your non-writing hand to write a letter or using your non-dominant hand to paint your nails. These things are uncomfortable to do at first, but over time, with lots of practice, you will eventually be able to do it with less discomfort. One day, it is going to be natural and automatic for you.

Another example of how this would work in a real-life setting can be connected to the practice of the law of attraction, which states that what you send out will come back to you. Thus, if you are sending out negative energy, then you will receive negative energy. Imagine that you are in a stressful situation and instead of using negative-irrational thoughts, you use positive-rational thoughts; see how the energy in the environment changes. You will, over time, start to draw in more positive thoughts and energy, and with this positive-energy shift within your life, you will be able to start living a much happier, healthier life.

Conclusion

Thank you for making it through to the end of *Cognitive Behavioral Therapy*. Let's hope it was as informative as it needed to be to inspire big changes in your life. I also hope that we were able to provide you with all of the tools you need to achieve your goals for any mental health conditions that have been plaguing you and preventing you from living a healthy life.

The next step in your healing process is to do some more research on therapists that practice cognitive behavioral therapy. Then find a certified therapist who is right for your needs. When working with a therapist, inform them of your negative thought patterns and what it is you wish to change about yourself. Remember that staying in the moment is important for identifying the emotions connected to the thoughts that are limiting your ability to live a happy life.

Many tools and techniques have been extensively studied for effectively dealing with mental health issues. Cognitive behavioral therapy is the most widely used form of treatment because of its effectiveness with many conditions. Since you are reading this, I assume you have decided to take the first step to getting your mental health back on track.

97

Congratulations on finding this highly effective way to help yourself heal your mental health, as well as finding an alternative for the irrational-negative thoughts that have been limiting your happiness. By changing them to more rational-positive thoughts, you can begin changing your life for the better.

Finally, if you found this book useful in any way, a review on Amazon is always appreciated!